Well Dressed: Salad Dressings

Jeff Keys

Photographs by
Zac Williams

GIBBS SMITH
TO ENRICH AND INSPIRE HUMANKIND

This book is dedicated to my mom and dad,
Barbara and Barney Keys,
who always got excited over something good to eat.

First Edition
15 14 13 12 11   5 4 3 2 1

Text © 2011 Jeff Keys
Photographs © 2011 Zac Williams

Published by
Gibbs Smith
P.O. Box 667
Layton, Utah 84041

1.800.835.4993 orders
www.gibbs-smith.com

Designed by Sugar Design
Printed and bound in Hong Kong
Gibbs Smith books are printed on paper produced
from sustainable PEFC-certified forest/controlled
wood source. Learn more at www.pefc.org.

Library of Congress Cataloging-in-Publication Data

Keys, Jeff.
  Well dressed : salad dressings / Jeff Keys ;
photographs by Zac Williams.
    p. cm.
  Includes index.
  ISBN 978-1-4236-1766-2
  1. Salad dressing. 2. Cookbooks. I. Williams, Zac.
II. Title.
  TX819.S27K49 2011
  641.8'14—dc22
                                        2010034831

CONTENTS

· ·

INTRODUCTION

WELCOME TO MY WORLD of salad dressings. *Well Dressed: Salad Dressings* is dedicated to taking you on a journey into the heart and soul of a great salad. And make no mistake, it is the dressing that gives a salad its soul.

The cycle of the seasons here in Sun Valley, Idaho, is a most fitting metaphor for my world of salad dressings. At Vintage Restaurant, I whisk up dressings year-round using seasonal ingredients, re-creating flavors from around the world. Dressings can transport you through every season and carry you to far-off places and cultures through their many diverse ingredients and surprising combinations of color, texture, flavor and temperature.

To flesh out the whole international culture idea, variety comes front and center. Oils and vinegars are the star players. Hearty and fruity extra virgin olive oil from Italy and France make the most classic vinaigrettes. Mellower and less expensive versions of olive oil that come from Spain and Greece work well also. It's really a matter of tasting a variety of olive oils to discover which ones you like the best. More common oils like canola, sunflower seed, and safflower work

great also. And there is a new kid on the block: grapeseed oil. I love it—mild and fruity in flavor, it is another ingredient of the highly respected Mediterranean diet.

Now for the vinegar. It brings a kind of life force, an electricity, to the vinaigrette. Get to know different vinegars by tasting them. Come to realize their power. Red wine, white wine, sherry, apple cider vinegar, rice, balsamic—each one has it's own distinctive personality and character.

Salad dressings are so taken for granted. Given the dozens of commercial salad dressings available in every supermarket and grocery store, it's so easy to simply open a bottled dressing without even thinking about it. In fact, I have a handful of favorites that I use in combination with other ingredients to give them a lift. But making your own salad dressing at home is the idea I want to put into your mind. It starts out so simply and easily: drizzle a little olive oil and a few drops of red wine vinegar over some super-fresh salad greens and vine-ripened sliced tomatoes, sprinkle some fresh snipped herbs in there too. *Voila!* A fresh and fabulous homemade salad dressing. It is so delicious and fast and fun! Plus, you control the ingredients, all healthy and fresh. I believe that is an important concept—taking control of what and how you eat. One element in taking control of your own life.

A great friend and early mentor in the food world, David Batterson, clued me in to this idea early in my food career. He had invited me to his house for dinner, the first time a great chef had ever done that for me. I was young, highly impressionable and a bit nervous. David was one of the great chefs in Aspen, Colorado, in the years before celebrity TV chefs. He had cooked at Aspen's finest restaurant of the era, The Copper Kettle, and was the head chef of Aspen's wildest restaurant, Andre's. I worked under David at both restaurants and what a wild ride it was. I looked up to David because he was a smart, cagey and loving wild man who showed me the potential of living the good life with inspiration from music,

literature and fascinating people—some of whom, like James Beard, Alan Ginsberg and Miles Davis, and Zorba the Greek became important mentors in my own life. That night at dinner, David started things off with a simple salad of leafy greens with a drizzle of extra virgin olive oil and a squeeze of fresh lemon juice. It was simplicity magnified and was the best salad I had ever eaten! The explosion of flavors, the binding of the salad ingredients by the dressing created an experience I'll never forget—my mouth waters just writing about it.

The chemistry of a good salad dressing hits the pleasure centers of your brain immediately. There is no waiting around for the effect. The acid element—vinegar or citrus juice—lights the fuse. A lush vegetable oil carries the flavors of spice and herb or garlic directly to the sensory receptors of your mouth.

These days, salads have become much more than just a course in a larger meal. They often become the meal itself. A good salad and some warm bread make for good eating. Sometimes that is all you need. Better yet, combining the cool, crunchy ingredients of a salad with a warm ingredient like crispy roasted potatoes or slices of juicy roasted chicken or grilled steak makes for a healthy, satisfying meal. And what brings all of these elements together and makes them so appealing? It's the dressing. *The dressing is the liaison that makes it all work*. The ingredients in the dressing work like healthy stimulants, waking up our appetite for excitement and well-being.

The Chinese call the creative source in our body and spirit the "hollow bamboo." It describes the infinite well of our creativity, and the ingredients in salad dressings give nourishment to that mystical reservoir. There is a reason old-time medicines included vinegars, olive oil, garlic, fresh herbs and honey as homespun remedies: these ingredients turn the immune system to the "on" position and kick out the evil spirits! Vinegars in ancient cultures were used for medicinal purposes to relieve ailing joints, to invigorate the immune system and to improve skin and hair quality. Honey was, and is, used to cleanse wounds as a natural antibiotic, to soothe digestive problems and to kick up energy. Garlic has long been

thought of as a natural elixir to relieve intestinal problems, to prevent colds and sore throats and, who can forget, as a protection against vampires (just kidding). Then there are the endless healing and protective qualities of olive oil. Just sip a spoonful of good extra virgin olive oil and you can intuitively feel its power.

By combining these amazing ingredients to make a salad dressing, you create an alchemy of healthy eating, which, I believe, helps to create a confident approach to living.

My goal in *Well Dressed* is to inspire you to try these salad dressings at home and come to enjoy making them. I hope that you find a dressing or vinaigrette—or many—that you really like and incorporate into your own cooking repertoire. I present these recipes and ideas to begin a fine collaboration in good eating. I wish you well in your discoveries and hope you enjoy the book and fall in love all over again with good taste and the freedom of discovery.

Happy eating.

—Jeff Keys
Sun Valley, Idaho

VINAIGRETTES

SIMPLICITY AND VARIETY are the themes I want to communicate about the world of vinaigrette salad dressings. It's easy to start. All you need are good vegetable oil and a little vinegar. In fact, I'll bet you could make a vinaigrette right now. Just look in your pantry and find a bottle of olive oil or canola oil, a small bottle of red wine vinegar, some dry whole leaf thyme. You have salt—sea salt I hope—and a pepper grinder. Is there a garlic clove handy?

Let's make vinaigrette with just these ingredients, enough for two salads. First, smash the garlic clove on a cutting board and finely mince it. Put the garlic into a small mixing bowl. Now add 1 tablespoon of your vinegar, a pinch of salt and freshly ground black pepper; add a hearty pinch of the whole leaf thyme. Whisk in 3 tablespoons of your salad oil and you are done. You can use this vinaigrette right now, or cover it and save it for later. It couldn't be simpler and only took a minute.

The recipes here feature combinations of vinegar and oil along with an amazing array of herbs, citrus, seeds, nuts, and other ingredients to enhance your salads. Have fun!

Texas Hill Country Vinaigrette

This one goes great with slivered jicama, orange, grapefruit, and avocado salad. It's also terrific drizzled over shredded lettuce salad placed on top of a steamy hot quesadilla.

Makes about 1 cup

¼ cup red wine vinegar
1 tablespoon honey
1 teaspoon New Mexico chili powder
½ teaspoon freshly ground fennel seeds
1 small pinch cayenne pepper

Kosher salt and freshly ground
    black pepper to taste
1 tablespoon freshly snipped cilantro,
    basil, or mint (optional)
½ cup light olive oil, or a blend of ¼ cup
    olive oil and ¼ cup canola oil

To make the vinaigrette

Combine all of the ingredients except the oil in a bowl and blend evenly. Now drizzle in the oil and whisk a little to blend the flavors. Store in a covered glass jar in the fridge.

Fire-Roasted Green Chili Vinaigrette

This dressing captures the pungent and tangy flavors of the Southwest. I love to drizzle it over luscious street tacos.

Makes about 1¼ cups

½ cup diced fire-roasted green Anaheim chilies (about 2 to 3 chilies)	⅛ teaspoon freshly ground black pepper
¼ cup olive oil	1 pinch kosher salt to taste
¼ cup canola oil	1 teaspoon honey
4 cloves garlic	1 tablespoon freshly squeezed lime juice
	⅓ cup seasoned rice vinegar

To make the vinaigrette

To roast the chilies, preheat oven to 450 degrees F. Lightly oil an ovenproof sauté pan and place over medium-high heat; gently place the Anaheim chilies in the pan. Be careful not to splatter the hot oil. Turning the chilies, blacken the skins on all sides and then put the pan in the oven for about 6 minutes. Remove the chilies to a paper towel and let them cool.

Once the chilies are cool, rub off the blackened skins and then rinse and dry the chilies. Now cut off the stem, cut the chilies in half, remove the seeds, and cut the chilies into small dice.

To finish the vinaigrette, put the oils and the garlic in the sauté pan and heat the oil to a slow simmer; cook the garlic for about 6 minutes. It should just barely turn golden. Now let the oil cool for about 10 minutes. Discard 2 of the garlic cloves, then place the remaining oil and garlic in a blender with all other ingredients. Put on the lid and process at a medium speed for about 20 seconds.

Fire-Roasted Red Bell Pepper and Braised Garlic Vinaigrette

This simple variation gives you a whisper of the flavors of the Mediterranean.

Makes about 1¼ cups

½ cup diced fire-roasted red bell
    pepper (about 2 peppers)
¼ cup olive oil
¼ cup canola oil
4 cloves garlic

1 teaspoon honey
⅛ teaspoon freshly ground black pepper
1 pinch kosher salt to taste
1 pinch cayenne pepper
⅓ cup red wine vinegar

To make the vinaigrette

To roast the red bell peppers, preheat oven to 450 degrees F. Lightly oil the peppers and place them on a sheet pan. Roast them in the oven for about 15 minutes, turning them twice for even cooking. The skins should be turning black and separating from the pepper.

While the peppers are roasting, heat the oils in a sauté pan. Add garlic and cook at a slow simmer for about 6 minutes. The garlic should just be turning a light golden color and should be soft and buttery.

Remove the peppers from the oven and seal in a paper bag for about 15 minutes. They will become soft as they cool. Peel the skin off the peppers and discard; rinse and dry the peppers. Remove the stem, cut peppers in half, remove the seeds, and dice the flesh.

Finish the vinaigrette by putting all of the ingredients except 2 garlic cloves (discard these) into a blender and process the vinaigrette with the lid on at medium speed for 20 seconds. Taste for seasoning. Store in a covered glass jar in fridge.

Mango, Sweet Onion, and Fresh Thyme Vinaigrette

This one is from a white sand beach on a turquoise bay in the Caribbean.

Makes about 1⅓ cups

⅓ cup seasoned rice vinegar
1 tablespoon freshly squeezed lime juice
1 clove garlic, smashed and finely diced
1½ teaspoons honey
1 tablespoon fresh thyme leaves
1 tablespoon plus 1 teaspoon finely
    diced sweet red onion

1 finely diced seeded jalapeno pepper
½ cup ¼-inch-dice ripe mango
1 pinch sea salt to taste
⅛ teaspoon freshly ground black pepper
½ cup light olive oil

To make the vinaigrette

In a mixing bowl, add all of the ingredients except the oil. Stir to blend them evenly. While stirring with a wire whip, drizzle in the oil. Stores well in a covered glass jar in the fridge.

Sesame Mint Vinaigrette

Exotic flavors from steamy street markets from Marseille to Morocco.

Makes about 1¼ cups

3 tablespoons red wine vinegar
3 tablespoons seasoned rice vinegar
2 teaspoons brown sugar
¼ teaspoon kosher salt
1 tablespoon finely grated orange zest
½ teaspoon whole fennel seeds

1 teaspoon freshly grated ginger
1–2 tablespoons fresh mint leaves,
  crushed then chopped
1 tablespoon plus 1 teaspoon lightly
  toasted sesame seeds
½ cup light olive oil

To make the vinaigrette

Add all the ingredients in the order given
to a mixing bowl. Blend well and chill.
Store in a covered glass jar in the fridge.

Wine Country Honey-Roasted Grape Vinaigrette

Serving a salad with this dressing is a wonderful surprise in mid-winter.
Takes you right back to the brilliance of a summer day in the vineyard.
And in summer it's always a joy!

Makes about 1 cup

1½ tablespoons red or white wine vinegar
1 tablespoon honey
½ cup small red grapes (if grapes are large, halve them before measuring)
1 tablespoon freshly squeezed orange juice

1 medium-size clove garlic, smashed and finely minced
¼ cup extra virgin olive oil
Small pinch kosher salt
Pinch freshly ground black pepper

To make the vinaigrette

Preheat your oven to 350 degrees. Into a small non-corrosive saute pan, put the vinegar, honey and grapes. Put in the oven and roast for about 10 minutes. The grapes will start to plump up and all the flavors will combine beautifully.

While grapes are roasting, squeeze orange juice into a bowl. Add the garlic and swirl around to bring out the flavor.

When the grapes are finished roasting, swirl the grape mixture into the orange juice. Now swirl in the oil and add the salt and pepper.

The dressing is great served warm but also wonderful served chilled. It's also fun to substitute blueberries for the grapes—fabulous flavors. Keep covered in the refrigerator and use within 5 days.

Super-Quick Honey-Lemon-Thyme Vinaigrette

You can also substitute fresh rosemary leaves for the fresh thyme leaves in this recipe.

Makes about 1 cup

1 clove garlic, smashed and minced
1 teaspoon dry mustard powder
1 tablespoon fresh thyme leaves
1 tablespoon honey
3 tablespoons freshly squeezed lemon juice

⅛ teaspoon kosher salt
⅛ teaspoon freshly ground black pepper
½ cup extra virgin olive oil (for a milder flavor, use ¼ cup olive oil and ¼ cup canola oil)

To make the vinaigrette

Put all the ingredients except the oil in a mixing bowl and swirl around with a wire whip to blend and dissolve the honey.

Continue swirling and drizzle in the oil. Shake well before serving. Stores well in a covered glass jar in the fridge.

Variation: Super-Quick Honey-Lemon-Parsley Vinaigrette

A great last-minute dressing featuring the underappreciated parsley.

Make the vinaigrette, but substitute 1 teaspoon Dijon mustard for the dry mustard powder and 1½ tablespoons finely chopped fresh parsley for the fresh thyme leaves.

Honey-Roasted Raspberry Vinaigrette

In early summer, lush, fat raspberries are ripening here in Sun Valley, Idaho. It's one of my favorite times of year. The fresh produce is coming on and I look forward each day to seeing what new fresh ingredients I can add to my cooking at the restaurant. The fresh herbs are young and tender, so it's time to make a great salad dressing combining fresh raspberries with fresh tarragon.

Makes about 3/4 cup

1½ tablespoons red wine vinegar
1 tablespoon honey
⅓ cup fresh raspberries
1 tablespoon freshly squeezed orange juice
1 tablespoon freshly snipped tarragon leaves

1 medium-size clove garlic, smashed and finely minced
¼ cup extra virgin olive oil
Very small pinch kosher salt
Pinch freshly ground black pepper

To make the vinaigrette

Preheat your oven to 350 degrees. Put the vinegar, honey and raspberries into a non-corrosive saute pan. Place in oven and roast for 10 minutes.

While the raspberries are roasting, combine orange juice, tarragon and garlic in a small bowl and swirl a little to bring out the flavors. When the raspberries have finished roasting, combine the raspberry mixture with the orange juice mixture. Now swirl in the olive oil. Then swirl in the salt and pepper.

The dressing is delicious served right away, while it is warm, but also good served chilled. Keeps in the fridge, covered. Best served within 5 days for the freshest flavor. The recipe is easily doubled if you want more.

Orange Pecan Vinaigrette

This is one of my all-time favorite vinaigrettes. It's healthy for you, it's easy to make, and it's very delicious. Try it tossed with bib lettuce, fresh pear slices, and a great gorgonzola cheese.

Makes 1 cup

3 tablespoons seasoned rice vinegar
⅓ cup orange blossom honey
1 teaspoon freshly grated orange zest
3 tablespoons freshly squeezed orange juice
1 pinch kosher salt to taste

1 pinch freshly ground black pepper to taste
½ cup light olive oil, or a blend of ¼ cup olive oil and ¼ cup canola oil
⅓ cup lightly toasted chopped pecans

To make the vinaigrette

Add all the ingredients except the oil and pecans to a mixing bowl and whisk with a wire whip until honey has dissolved and blended with the other ingredients. Now drizzle in the oil, continuing to stir until blended. Add the toasted pecans. Stores well in the fridge in a covered glass jar.

Intense Citrus and Fresh Thyme Vinaigrette

This dressing is appealing for its intense concentration of citrus flavors combined with the mellow touch of honey and fresh thyme. It's wonderful on any green salad and reaches perfection when drizzled over a warm sliced beet and goat cheese salad.

Makes about 1 cup

⅓ cup freshly squeezed lemon juice
⅓ cup freshly squeezed grapefruit juice
⅓ cup freshly squeezed orange juice
1 tablespoon finely diced sweet red onion
2 teaspoons honey
2 teaspoons Dijon mustard

1 teaspoon fresh thyme leaves
1 pinch kosher salt to taste
1 pinch freshly ground black pepper to taste
¼ cup extra virgin olive oil
¼ cup canola oil

To make the vinaigrette

Add the three citrus juices to a small saucepan and reduce the mixture to ⅓ cup over medium-high heat. Remove from heat and add the onion and honey; let the mixture cool. Pour into a small mixing bowl and swirl in the mustard and thyme. Season with salt and pepper. Now whisk in the oils. Stores well in a covered glass jar in the fridge.

Fresh Basil Vinaigrette for Three-Bean Salad

These flavors are a perfect blend for three-bean or similar salads. Let your imagination be your guide. And the flavors only get better after a day in the fridge.

Makes about 1 cup

1 clove garlic, smashed and minced
2 teaspoons Dijon mustard
¼ cup white wine vinegar
1 teaspoon sugar
1 pinch kosher salt to taste

⅛ teaspoon freshly ground black pepper
¼ cup fresh basil, finely chopped
¼ cup extra virgin olive oil
¼ cup canola oil

To make the vinaigrette

Add all the ingredients except the oil to a mixing bowl and use a small wire whip to stir the mixture. This will bruise the basil leaves, which will release their flavor. Drizzle in the oil and stir just to blend.

The vinaigrette is ready to pour over a three-bean salad. Add some thinly sliced onions to the mixture for an extra layer of flavor. Stores well in the fridge in a glass jar with a lid.

Warm Mushroom, Bacon, and Molasses Vinaigrette

This is another warm dressing that I love. It's great served with a salad of spinach, warm sliced beets, and goat cheese or simply spooned over a great steak and some country-fried potatoes.

Makes about 1¼ cups

3 thick-cut slices smoked bacon
2 tablespoons reserved bacon drippings
3 tablespoons finely diced shallot
1½ cups sliced baby shiitake mushroom
    or small crimini mushrooms
¼ cup white wine vinegar

1 tablespoon molasses
1 teaspoon soy sauce
1 tablespoon fresh thyme leaves
¼ teaspoon freshly ground black pepper
½ cup mild olive oil, or a blend of ¼ cup
    olive oil and ¼ cup canola oil

To make the vinaigrette

Cook the bacon till just slightly crisp and remove to paper towels; pat dry to remove the excess bacon fat. Reserve the bacon drippings from the pan. Next sauté the shallots and mushrooms in 2 tablespoons of the reserved bacon drippings for about 3 minutes.

Add the vinegar, molasses, soy sauce, thyme, and pepper to the sautéed mushrooms. Bring to a simmer and cook for 1 minute. Remove from heat and whisk in the oil.

The vinaigrette is perfect to serve right now. It also stores nicely in the fridge to warm up later and is also really good served cold or at room temperature.

Warm Celeriac and Lemon Vinaigrette

Celeriac is a wonderful root vegetable whose gnarly appearance on the outside disguises the delicious vegetable inside. It tastes a bit like celery (of course) but with a nutty quality. When it is sautéed, roasted, or fried, a wonderful nutty, creamy taste complements the mild celery flavor. I love the contrast of warm dressings over cool salads.

Makes about 1¼ cups

⅓ cup mild olive oil
1 large celeriac bulb, peeled and cut into ¼-inch dice (about 1 cup)
2 tablespoons rice wine vinegar

2 tablespoons freshly squeezed lemon juice
1 pinch kosher salt to taste
1 pinch freshly grated black pepper
2 tablespoons snipped fresh chervil

To make the vinaigrette

In a medium-sized sauté pan, add the olive oil and sauté the diced celeriac on low to medium heat until tender. Remove the sauté pan from heat and let cool a little.

Stir the vinegar and lemon juice into the sautéed celeriac and season with salt and pepper. Taste for seasoning and adjust to your preference. Add the chervil. Just before serving reheat the vinaigrette and serve. This vinaigrette is great with cool, crispy green salads or as the dressing for a warm potato salad. Try tossing it with some greens and serve it with grilled fresh fish. This vinaigrette is best to use when freshly made.

Fresh Tarragon and Citrus Trio Vinaigrette

The Southern California coastline is the Mediterranean of the United States. Citrus trees and fresh herbs grow there as they do in the Mediterranean region. My mom's garden and flower borders on the coast were filled with fresh herb plants of every sort. Citrus trees and avocado trees were laid out like a French farm orchard. Nearby was an old woodpile. As a kid I hung out back there, feeling like I was in another world. This vinaigrette is for Mom, who passed on her love of the garden and of good food to me.

Makes about 1 cup

1 tablespoon freshly squeezed orange juice
1 tablespoon freshly squeezed lime juice
1 tablespoon freshly squeezed lemon juice
1 tablespoon white wine vinegar
2 teaspoons Dijon mustard
2 teaspoons honey

2 tablespoons chopped fresh tarragon leaves
1/8 teaspoon freshly ground black pepper
1 pinch kosher salt to taste
2 tablespoons hazelnut oil
1/4 cup extra virgin olive oil
1/4 cup canola oil

To make the vinaigrette

Add all the ingredients except the oil in a mixing bowl, whisking to blend evenly and to dissolve the honey. While whisking, drizzle in the oils to combine everything evenly. Stores well in a covered glass jar in the fridge.

Toasted Walnut and Blue Cheese Vinaigrette

What a nice surprise combination of flavors! The creamy and bold blue cheese, the toasted walnuts, the electricity of lemon, and the oil to mellow it all out. Try it with a beet and spinach salad. Or spoon a little over a seared black pepper–infused rib eye steak. Or just toss some with your favorite mixed greens. It's great!

Makes about 1¼ cups

2 tablespoons freshly squeezed lemon juice
1 tablespoon red wine vinegar
2 tablespoons diced fresh chives
1 clove garlic, smashed and minced
⅛ teaspoon freshly ground black pepper

1 pinch kosher salt
¼ cup walnut oil
¼ cup canola oil
½ cup toasted walnuts, coarsely chopped
½ cup blue cheese crumbles

To make the vinaigrette

Add the first 6 ingredients in a mixing bowl, whisking to evenly blend. Now drizzle in the oils and blend. Gently stir in the blue cheese and the chopped walnuts.

Stores well in a covered glass jar in the fridge. Use this vinaigrette within 2 to 3 days before the walnuts go soft.

INTERNATIONAL

COOKING AT ITS BEST is always a trip around the world, and as you wander through this book, you'll see that my influences come from every corner of the planet. I've always loved the food world for that.

I think the goal of every chef must be to capture a taste, a moment in time that paints a picture and gives someone a memorable experience. You want people to say, "Wow! That was great!"

So, now let's start a vinaigrette world tour. We focus on salad dressing recipes that define a culture's traditions using ingredients that fill a people's collective memory, that they in turn use to tell the rest of the world exactly who they are. We, the people of the world, do that all the time with our food, music and literature. In the end, it's an amazing discovery to realize that we know these ingredients. Like a song, they are floating around in the air until we capture them in a recipe and turn them into something fun and exciting. Hey, I'm hungry. Let's eat!

A Paris Bistro Vinaigrette

This is the first salad dressing that I saw a real French chef make. It was at Le Cheminee Restaurant in Aspen, Colorado. It was a brand-new restaurant and hadn't even opened yet. Hopes were high and a vibrant frantic current ran through the kitchen as preparations were made for the first busy night. Would we be ready? French was the only language spoken and I was a bit lost. But my eyes were open and I learned through hand signals, tone of voice (mostly a high-pitched wail), and blind luck. This vinaigrette tastes like a backstreet French bistro. Here is my version of the classic.

Makes about 1 cup

1 fresh egg yolk*
1 tablespoon Dijon mustard
1 clove garlic, smashed and minced
1 tablespoon freshly squeezed lemon juice
1 heaping teaspoon chopped
   fresh tarragon leaves

1 pinch kosher salt
   Freshly ground black pepper to taste
¼ cup extra virgin olive oil
¼ cup canola oil

To make the vinaigrette

Put all ingredients except the oils into a mixing bowl and blend evenly and gently with a wire whip. Now, still stirring with the wire whip, drizzle in the oils in a light stream. The egg mixture will absorb the oil and you will end up with a very light emulsion that makes a delicious dressing. You can substitute white wine vinegar, tarragon vinegar, or red wine vinegar for the lemon juice. Try different oils also. Hazelnut oil or walnut oil work great. Stores in a tightly covered container in the fridge for 1 week.

*Substitute pasteurized egg yolk if you wish.

Asian Red Dragon Beet Vinaigrette

It's a wonderful discovery to see how well beets combine with Asian flavors to make an unusual and delicious vinaigrette.

Makes about 1¹/₂ cups

¼ cup olive oil
¼ cup canola oil
1 teaspoon toasted sesame oil
4 cloves peeled garlic
½ cup diced tender cooked red beets
⅛ teaspoon freshly ground black pepper

1 pinch kosher salt to taste
1 teaspoon Asian Sriracha hot sauce
1 teaspoon freshly grated ginger
1 teaspoon honey
⅓ cup seasoned rice vinegar

To make the vinaigrette

Add the oils and the garlic cloves in a small saucepan. Heat the oil to a slow simmer and braise the garlic for about 6 minutes; the garlic should just barely turn golden. Discard 3 of the cloves of garlic. Let the oil cool for about 10 minutes.

Put the remaining garlic clove, oil, and all of the remaining ingredients into a blender. Process with the lid on at medium speed for about 20 seconds. Stores well in the fridge in a tightly covered container for 2 weeks.

Asian Golden Dragon Beet Vinaigrette

This dressing is so easy. Simply substitute golden beets for the red beets in the Asian Red Dragon Vinaigrette.

Makes about 1½ cups

1 recipe Asian Red Dragon Beet Vinaigrette (page 34)

½ cup diced tender cooked golden beets

To make the vinaigrette

In a bowl, combine all of the ingredients except the oil and blend evenly. Now drizzle in the oil and whisk a little to blend the flavors. Store in a covered glass jar in the fridge. Stores well in the fridge in a tightly covered container for 2 weeks.

Farmers-Style French Vinaigrette

Out in the countryside, the vinaigrette is a little heartier. Here is one to try.

Makes about 1 cup

1 fresh egg yolk*
1 tablespoon coarse country mustard
1 clove garlic, smashed and minced
1 tablespoon red wine vinegar
1 tablespoon chopped parsley

1 pinch kosher salt
 Freshly ground black pepper to taste
½ cup olive oil blend
1 fresh hard-boiled egg, chopped

To make the vinaigrette

In a mixing bowl add all ingredients except the oil and hard-boiled egg and stir gently with a wire whip until evenly blended. While stirring with the whip, slowly drizzle in the oil. The egg mixture will absorb the oil and you will end up with a light emulsion. Now gently blend in the chopped hard-boiled egg. Keep in the fridge in a tightly covered container for 1 week.

*Substitute pasteurized egg yolk if you wish.

Simple Spanish Sherry Vinaigrette

Sherry vinegar is a more potent and alive version of red wine vinegar. This simple recipe is very similar to the Simple Italian Balsamic Vinaigrette on page 45. That's about the easiest way I know to get from Italy to Spain!

Makes about 1¾ cups

1 cup light olive oil
8 cloves garlic

2 teaspoons honey
¾ cup sherry vinegar

To make the vinaigrette

Put the olive oil in a small sauté pan with the garlic cloves. Heat the oil to a slow simmer and braise the garlic for about 6 minutes. It will just begin to turn golden. Remove the pan from the heat and let the oil cool down. Remove the garlic and discard.

In a small bowl, dissolve the honey in the balsamic vinegar. Now add the garlic oil and blend.

This simple vinaigrette is delicious. Stores well in a covered glass jar in the fridge.

Paris Bistro Vinaigrette, Asian-Style

This dressing is a Paris Bistro construction but with Asian flavors. I serve it with a thinly sliced Chinese cabbage salad tossed with warm toasted sourdough bread croutons to absorb the dressing. Add steamed sugar snap peas, bean sprouts, and freshly snipped chervil to the salad. It's delicious.

Makes about 1 cup

1 fresh egg yolk*
1 tablespoon Dijon mustard
1 clove garlic, smashed and minced
1 tablespoon seasoned rice vinegar
1 tablespoon toasted sesame seeds
2 tablespoons chopped green onions

1 pinch kosher salt
1 pinch freshly ground black pepper
¼ cup olive oil
¼ cup canola oil
1 teaspoon toasted sesame oil

To make the vinaigrette

Add all ingredients except the oils to a mixing bowl and blend evenly and gently with a wire whip. Now, while stirring with the whip, drizzle in the oils in a light stream. The egg mixture will absorb the oils and you will end up with a very light emulsion that makes a very nice dressing. Enjoy! Stores in a tightly covered container in the fridge for 1 week.

*Substitute pasteurized egg yolk if you wish.

Asian Herb Trio Vinaigrette

Many cultures use cilantro, basil and mint in their cooking. Tweaking these ingredients with a little rice vinegar, sesame oil and fresh ginger captures the essence of Asian cooking.

Makes about 1 cup

- ¼ cup olive oil
- ¼ cup canola oil
- 1 teaspoon toasted sesame oil
- 4 cloves peeled garlic
- ⅛ teaspoon freshly ground black pepper
- 1 pinch kosher salt to taste
- 1 teaspoon freshly grated ginger
- 1 teaspoon honey

- 1 tablespoon plus 1 teaspoon chopped fresh cilantro
- 1 tablespoon plus 1 teaspoon chopped fresh mint
- 1 tablespoon plus 1 teaspoon chopped fresh basil
- 1 teaspoon freshly squeezed lime juice
- ⅓ cup seasoned rice vinegar

To make the vinaigrette

Add the oils and the garlic cloves in a small saucepan. Heat the oil to a slow simmer and braise the garlic for about 6 minutes. The garlic should just barely turn golden. Discard 3 of the garlic cloves. Put the remaining garlic clove, oil, and all of the ingredients into a blender; process with the lid on at a medium speed for about 20 seconds. The vinaigrette is ready. Stores well in the fridge in a tightly covered container for 2 weeks.

Asian Peanut Street Stand Dressing

The quintessential Asian street vendor dressing is all about bright flavors and mouthwatering goodness, and this one has it all in one compact package. This one is so good tossed with Chinese egg noodles and served over a bowl of greens like bok choy and Chinese cabbage that are drizzled with nuoc cham. Throw in some sliced grilled chicken or pork and you'll have a great street vendor feast.

Makes about 1¹/₂ cups

1 tablespoon finely grated ginger
2 tablespoons freshly squeezed lime juice
2 tablespoons balsamic vinegar
1 tablespoon brown sugar
2 tablespoons chopped cilantro
¹/₈ teaspoon fresh ground black pepper
2 tablespoons finely diced shallots

1 tablespoon soy sauce
1 tablespoon Asian fish sauce
2 medium-size cloves garlic, smashed
1 teaspoon toasted sesame oil
4–5 tablespoons creamy peanut butter
³/₄ cup light salad oil
2 tablespoons water

To make the dressing

Place all of the ingredients in a food processor and pulse the processor until the ingredients are evenly blended. If the dressing is too thick, add another tablespoon of water. Keeps in fridge, covered, for up to 5 days.

Sesame Seed Vinaigrette

This vinaigrette is fantastic to drizzle over green salad mixes to add an Asian accent.

Makes about 2 cups

1 cup light olive oil
1 tablespoon sesame oil
8 cloves garlic
2 teaspoons honey
1 tablespoon mirin

3/4 cup seasoned rice vinegar
2 tablespoons lightly toasted sesame seeds
2 tablespoons thinly sliced green onions
1 pinch red chili flakes
6 fresh basil leaves, thinly sliced

To make the vinaigrette

Put the oils and the garlic cloves in a small saucepan. Heat the oil to a slow simmer and braise the garlic for about 6 minutes. It should just be turning a light golden color. Remove from heat and discard the garlic cloves.

In a small bowl, dissolve the honey in the mirin and vinegar. When the oil cools, add it to the vinegar mixture. Whisk the sesame seeds, green onions, chili flakes, and basil into oil and vinegar mixture.

Always shake this dressing to blend it evenly before serving. Stores well in the fridge in a tightly covered container for 2 weeks.

Simple Italian Balsamic Vinaigrette

This makes a great dressing for green salad or roasted veggies. It's also excellent drizzled over vine-ripened tomato slices or grilled mushrooms and onions.

Makes 1¾ cups

1 cup light olive oil	2 teaspoons honey
8 cloves garlic	¾ cup balsamic vinegar

To make the vinaigrette

Put the olive oil in a small sauté pan with the garlic cloves. Heat the oil to a slow simmer and braise the garlic for about 6 minutes. It will just begin to turn golden. Remove the pan from the heat and let the oil cool down. Remove the garlic and discard.

In a small bowl, dissolve the honey in the balsamic vinegar. Now add the garlic oil and blend. This simple vinaigrette is delicious. Stores well in a covered glass jar in the fridge.

Greek Pasta Salad Vinaigrette

This one goes great with any mixture of a Greek salad, including lots of tomatoes, greens, sliced onions, chopped veggies, Greek-style cured meats, and, of course, some fabulous pasta!

Makes about 2 cups

½ cup white wine vinegar
1 tablespoon Dijon mustard
3 cloves garlic, smashed and minced
2 teaspoons dry leaf oregano
¼ teaspoon kosher salt
¼ teaspoon freshly ground black pepper
1 teaspoon finely grated lemon zest
1 tablespoon freshly squeezed lemon juice

¼ cup snipped fresh young oregano leaves
¼ cup snipped fresh basil leaves
½ cup coarsely chopped sun-dried tomatoes (these come in a jar packed in oil), patted dry with paper towels
½ cup Greek crumbled feta cheese
½ cup pitted and halved Greek olives
1 cup extra virgin olive oil

To make the vinaigrette

Put all ingredients except the oil into a mixing bowl and whisk gently until evenly blended. Now drizzle in the olive oil continuing to whisk gently. Blend evenly before using. Store in the fridge in a covered glass jar and use during the first 2 or 3 days after making.

Chili-Lime Vinaigrette

Use this vinaigrette to add a Latin touch to any salad or grilled vegetable combination.

Makes about 1½ cups

4 tablespoons fresh lime juice
1 tablespoon sherry wine vinegar
   or red wine vinegar
2 cloves garlic, smashed and minced
2 tablespoons minced sweet red onion
2 tablespoons minced fresh cilantro
2 tablespoons minced fresh basil

¼ teaspoon cayenne pepper
1 teaspoon ground toasted cumin seeds
1½ fresh jalapeno peppers,
   stemmed and finely diced
¼ teaspoon kosher salt
¼ teaspoon freshly ground black pepper
1 cup extra virgin olive oil

To make the vinaigrette

Place all of the ingredients into a mixing bowl in the order listed. Blend evenly and serve.

This dressing is best served fresh but will store for a few days in a covered jar in the fridge.

A Simple Niçoise Vinaigrette

This vinaigrette gives you a taste of the South of France. It's great drizzled over a potato, tuna, green bean, and hard-cooked-egg salad. Try it on stacked sandwiches and all kinds of mixed green salads as well. Enjoy!

Makes about 1¼ cups

⅓ cup red wine vinegar	2 anchovy filets, chopped
1 clove garlic, smashed and minced	⅛ teaspoon freshly ground black pepper
2 teaspoons Dijon mustard	1 teaspoon finely chopped fresh parsley
½ teaspoon dry whole leaf thyme	¾ cup extra virgin olive oil

To make the vinaigrette

Add all the ingredients except the oil to a mixing bowl and whisk with a wire whip until well blended. Now blend in the olive oil. Stores well in a covered glass jar in the fridge.

Cabo San Lucas Street-Stand Vinaigrette

Wonderful drizzled over sliced vine-ripened tomatoes, sliced avocados, and thinly sliced sweet onions. Spoon it over spicy barbecued steak or chicken. It's great drizzled over homemade street-stand tacos as well.

Makes about 1 cup

- 2 tablespoons fresh lime juice
- 1 tablespoon fresh orange juice
- 1 tablespoon white wine vinegar
- 1 teaspoon smashed and minced garlic
- 2 tablespoons finely diced sweet red onion
- 2 tablespoons chopped fresh cilantro
- 1 pinch cayenne pepper
- ¼ teaspoon ground toasted cumin seeds
- ½ teaspoon kosher salt
- ⅛ teaspoon freshly ground black pepper
- ½ cup light olive oil, or blend of olive oil and canola oil to equal ½ cup

To make the vinaigrette

In a mixing bowl, blend all of the ingredients except the oil. Now drizzle in the oil, stir to blend the flavors, and the vinaigrette is ready. Stores great in the fridge in a covered glass jar.

Provencal Caper and Green Olive Vinaigrette

This vinaigrette is all about intense flavors. It's great drizzled over vine-ripened tomato slices with mozzarella and sliced sweet onions. Add a sprinkling of fresh basil and freshly ground black pepper. Or try this vinaigrette to dress a non-mayonnaise-based potato salad.

Makes about 1½ cups

¼ cup freshly squeezed grapefruit juice
2 tablespoons white wine vinegar
½ teaspoon dry mustard powder
½ teaspoon dry whole leaf thyme
1 tablespoon capers, patted dry
½ cup sliced green olives (Niçoise-style or pimento Martini olives), patted dry

2 tablespoons finely diced red or white onion
⅛ teaspoon freshly ground black pepper
¾ cup extra virgin olive oil (for a milder flavor, combine olive oil and canola oil to make ¾ cup)

To make the vinaigrette

In a mixing bowl, whisk together all the ingredients except the oil to evenly combine the flavors. Now whisk in the oil and it's ready. Stores well in a covered glass jar in the fridge.

Italian Pesto Vinaigrette

This vinaigrette works great for summer pasta salads. Try it with penne pasta, lots of tomatoes and kalamata olives, thin slices of fresh zucchini, and thinly sliced and then diced sweet red onion. It's delicious.

Makes about 2 cups

½ cup red wine vinegar
1 tablespoon Dijon mustard
2 teaspoons dry leaf basil
¼ teaspoon kosher salt to taste
¼ teaspoon freshly ground black pepper
1 teaspoon finely grated lemon zest
1 tablespoon freshly squeezed lemon juice

½ cup extra virgin olive oil
½ cup canola oil
½ cup freshly snipped basil leaves
¼ cup lightly toasted pine nuts
2 cloves garlic
½ cup grated Parmesan cheese

To make the vinaigrette

Put the first 7 ingredients into a mixing bowl and whisk with a wire whip to blend evenly. Now whisk in the oils. Put the last 4 ingredients into a food processor. Add about ⅓ cup of the prepared vinaigrette and process the mixture: pulse the processor off and on a few times until it is all blended. Now pour the processed mixture back into the vinaigrette, whisking to blend evenly. Chill in the fridge. Shake the vinaigrette well before using.

A Super-Quick Wasabi Vinaigrette

A great little taste of Japan here. This one is excellent with napa cabbage, bean sprouts, fresh herbs, bitter and sweet greens, rare seared tuna, sticky rice, or fresh cool greens over hot noodles. Whenever you want to explode flavor with a Japanese flair, try this one.

Makes about 1½ cups

- 4 teaspoons water
- 2 teaspoons wasabi powder
- 4 tablespoons rice vinegar
- 1 tablespoon freshly squeezed lime juice
- 2 cloves garlic, smashed and diced

- 2 teaspoons soy sauce
- 2 teaspoons Asian fish sauce
- 2 tablespoons diced green onions
- ²⁄₃ cup canola oil
- 1 teaspoon toasted sesame oil

To make the vinaigrette

In a mixing bowl, blend the water and the wasabi powder to form a paste. Now add the next 6 ingredients and whisk to blend evenly. When it is blended, drizzle the oils into the mixture while whisking. The vinaigrette is ready to serve. Stores in a tightly covered container in the fridge for 2 weeks.

Asian Ginger–Lime Vinaigrette

This is a nice refreshing vinaigrette that excels when tossed with blends of Asian greens and bean sprouts. Throw in some warm, freshly pan-seared croutons that are golden brown and crispy on the outside and soft and steamy on the inside. Make the croutons from good French bread, each about 1 inch square.

Makes about 1 1/2 cups

- 1 thumb-sized knob of fresh ginger, peeled and finely grated
- 2 tablespoons freshly squeezed lime juice
- 2 tablespoons seasoned rice vinegar
- 1 clove garlic, smashed and diced
- 2 teaspoons brown sugar
- 1 pinch cayenne
- 2 tablespoons freshly sliced mint leaves
- 2 tablespoons finely diced shallot
- 1 teaspoon soy sauce
- 2 teaspoons Asian fish sauce
- 1 teaspoon toasted sesame oil
- 1 cup light vegetable oil

To make the vinaigrette

Put all the ingredients except the oil into a mixing bowl and whisk until well blended. Now drizzle in the oil while whisking to blend evenly. Stores well in a covered glass jar in the fridge for up to a month.

SLAW AND CREAMY DRESSINGS

I LOVE COLESLAW any time of year. Hot or cold outside, it doesn't matter to me. In the summer, a good slaw is refreshing and adds a coolness to a meal that is so complementary to outdoor wood-fired or charcoal cooking. In the winter, I find a good slaw very complementary to hearty country-style cooking. Especially with a dish like country-fried pork chops that have been dusted with a spicy coating and fried to golden brown, served with some mashed potatoes and country gravy, the slaw adds a comforting element to the plate, always waking up the flavors of the other components. Another way I love to use a slaw is on sandwiches. They brighten and make the sandwich exciting. So here are a few of my favorite slaw dressings that are good to go year-round to make eating a lot of fun.

When you are in the mood for a salad version of dancing up close and slow, then a creamy dressing is what's called for. Where vinaigrettes will add exuberant sizzle to a salad, creamy dressings will be the embrace. They are the soft touch of the dressing world. Let's make a few and you will see what I'm talking about.

New Orleans Slaw Dressing

This dressing pays tribute to one of my favorite cities. A slaw with this dressing goes great with any kind of fish, chicken, pork, or beef cooked country style over wood or coals.

Makes about 2 cups

1½ cups mayonnaise
½ cup real apple cider vinegar*
⅓ cup sugar
1 to 2 teaspoons Vintage Spice Mix

VINTAGE SPICE MIX

2 tablespoons New Mexico chili powder
1 tablespoon Spanish paprika
1 tablespoon freshly ground black pepper
1 tablespoon kosher salt
1 tablespoon ground toasted cumin seed
1 tablespoon whole fennel seed
1 tablespoon curry powder
1 tablespoon whole leaf thyme
1 tablespoon cayenne
1 tablespoon onion powder
1 tablespoon granulated garlic

To make the dressing

Whisk all of the ingredients together in a bowl until evenly blended. Stores in a covered jar in the fridge for a week.

*Make sure it is not imitation apple cider vinegar!

To make the Vintage Spice Mix

Put the ingredients together in a bowl and evenly blend.

Poppy Seed Slaw Dressing

This one is simple and has all the basics of a great slaw dressing. It is sweet and sour, a little creamy, and with a little heat at the end. It is my kind of slaw dressing.

Makes about 2 ¼ cups

1½ cups mayonnaise
½ cup real apple cider vinegar*
⅓ cup sugar

1 tablespoon poppy seeds
1 pinch cayenne
⅛ teaspoon freshly ground black pepper

To make the dressing

Whisk all of the ingredients together in a bowl until evenly blended. You are ready to go. It's easy!

*Make sure it is not imitation apple cider vinegar! Rice vinegar also works well.

Caribbean Slaw Dressing

This is a fruity-tangy-spicy dressing from out island way. Try it with grated green papaya and shredded Chinese cabbage slaw. Be sure to throw in some thin-sliced sweet onion.

Makes about 1¼ cups

1 cup finely chopped mango
1 fresh jalapeno chili, finely chopped
¼ small habanero chili, seeded
   and very finely chopped
1 green onion, finely diced
¼ cup finely snipped cilantro

2 tablespoons freshly squeezed lime juice
2 tablespoons freshly squeezed orange juice
2 tablespoons sugar, to taste
3 tablespoons olive oil
3 tablespoons canola oil

To make the dressing

Add all ingredients except the oils to a mixing bowl and whisk together to blend evenly. Now drizzle in the oils while blending. Always shake the dressing to reblend before using. Stores well in the fridge in a covered glass jar.

Asian Slaw Dressing

After all of the Asian slaw dressings I have fooled around with over the years, it comes down to this little technique to make great Asian slaw. It's not really a dressing. It's just two little ingredients sprinkled over your Asian slaw mix.

Seasoned rice vinegar	Sugar

To make the dressing

Here's the technique. Add these veggies to your bowl of Asian slaw greens: thinly sliced Chinese or napa cabbage, thinly sliced cucumber, matchstick carrots, and fresh orange wedges. Over this mixture, simply drizzle a little seasoned rice vinegar, but not too much—just enough to lightly coat the greens. Then sprinkle on a little sugar. Again, not too much. You want it really light with a nice mellow touch of sweet and sour. Now toss the salad. That's it. Try it and experiment a little with it to get it just right.

Creamy Garlic Salad Dressing

This dressing is bold, garlicky, lemony, and delicious. It's also the dressing that is the base recipe of a whole slew of other creamy dressings. So let's start with this one.

Makes about 1½ cups

1 fresh egg yolk*	¼ cup extra virgin olive oil
1 tablespoon Dijon mustard	¾ cup canola oil
2 tablespoons freshly squeezed lemon juice	2 tablespoons sour cream
4–5 cloves peeled garlic, smashed and minced	¼ cup half-and-half
⅛ teaspoon freshly ground black pepper	Kosher salt to taste

To make the dressing

To the bowl of an electric mixer, add the first 5 ingredients. Turn the mixer to a medium speed and blend these ingredients. With the mixer still on medium, add the oils in a slow, steady stream. The egg yolk mixture will absorb the oils and make a nice emulsion that is like a mayonnaise. Now with the mixer on, add the sour cream, blend thoroughly, and then mix in the half-and-half.

Taste for salt. Add just a pinch or two to brighten the flavors of the dressing without tasting salty. The dressing should be a nice consistency that will blend with

salad ingredients. If it is too thick add a little more half-and-half. This dressing also works great drizzled back and forth over a wedge of lettuce with sliced tomato and sliced cucumber.

Here's one warning. This dressing is garlicky, just like I like it. But if it is too garlicky for you, feel free to use less garlic.

Store in a covered container in the fridge for up to 2 weeks.

*Substitute pasteurized egg yolk if you wish.

Creamy Blue Cheese Dressing

This is one of the best blue cheese dressings ever. Please, use a really good quality blue cheese, such as Roquefort, Stilton, or Gorgonzola when you make this dressing. It will be worth it.

Makes about 2 cups

1 fresh egg yolk*
1 tablespoon Dijon mustard
2 tablespoons freshly squeezed lemon juice
2–3 cloves garlic, smashed and diced
1/8 teaspoon freshly ground black pepper
1/4 cup extra virgin olive oil

3/4 cup canola oil
2 tablespoons sour cream
1/4 cup half-and-half
   Kosher salt to taste
1/2 cup crumbled blue cheese

To make the dressing

To the bowl of an electric mixer, add the egg yolk, mustard, lemon juice, garlic and pepper. Turn on the mixer to a medium speed and blend the ingredients. With the mixer still on medium, add the oils in a slow, steady stream. The egg yolk mixture will absorb the oils and make an emulsion that is like mayonnaise.

With the mixer still running, add the sour cream; blend thoroughly and mix in the half-and-half. Taste for salt; a pinch or two should brighten the flavor of the dressing without it tasting salty. Then gently blend

in the blue cheese. The dressing should be a consistency that will blend nicely with the salad ingredients. If it is too thick, add a little more half-and-half.

This dressing works great drizzled back and forth over a wedge of lettuce with sliced tomato and whatever other salad ingredients you enjoy. Stores nicely in the fridge, covered, for up to 2 weeks.

*Substitute pasteurized egg yolk if you wish.

Creamy Caesar Dressing

This is an especially good Caesar dressing. It's full bodied and luscious. Maybe it's not totally traditional but it has all of the proper elements. Enjoy!

Makes about 1½ cups

1 fresh egg yolk*
1 tablespoon Dijon mustard
2 tablespoons freshly squeezed lemon juice
2–3 peeled garlic cloves, smashed and minced
⅛ teaspoon freshly ground black pepper
2 canned or jarred anchovy fillets, patted dry and finely chopped
¼ cup extra virgin olive oil

¾ cup canola oil
2 tablespoons sour cream
¼ cup half-and-half
½ cup finely grated Parmesan cheese
1 extra tablespoon freshly squeezed lemon juice (optional)
2 hard-boiled eggs, chopped (optional)
1–2 pinches kosher salt to taste

To make the dressing

In the bowl of an electric mixer, add the first 6 ingredients. Turn on the mixer to a medium speed and blend the ingredients. With the mixer still on medium, drizzle in the oils in a light stream. The egg mixture will absorb the oils to make a mixture similar to a mayonnaise.

Blend in the sour cream, then the half-and-half, and then add the Parmesan. Blend thoroughly. Now add the extra tablespoon of lemon juice if you'd like the dressing a

little more lemony. If the dressing is too thick, add a little more half-and-half. Add a pinch of salt if needed.

Here is one more option I like. Add chopped hard-boiled eggs and blend into the dressing. It's yummy. This dressing is also great used as a dip. Stores up to 2 weeks in the fridge.

*Substitute pasteurized egg yolk if you wish.

Creamy Lemon, Fresh Tarragon, and Pink Peppercorn Dressing

This is my version of an old French Bistro dressing. It's all things French, from the lemon to the tarragon to the pink peppercorns. So enjoy a little side trip to France.

Makes about 1½ cups

1 fresh egg yolk*
1 tablespoon Dijon mustard
2 tablespoons freshly squeezed lemon juice
2 peeled cloves garlic, smashed and minced
⅛ teaspoon freshly ground black pepper
1 tablespoon plus 1 teaspoon dried
   whole pink peppercorns
1½ tablespoons chopped fresh tarragon leaves

¼ cup extra virgin olive oil
¾ cup canola oil
2 tablespoons sour cream
¼ cup half-and-half and ½ cup half-and-half
1 extra tablespoon freshly squeezed
   lemon juice (optional)
   Pinch kosher salt to taste

To make the dressing

In the bowl of an electric mixer add the first 7 ingredients. Turn on the mixer to medium and thoroughly blend. With the mixer still on medium, drizzle in the oils in a steady stream. The egg yolk mixture will absorb the oils and form an emulsion similar to a mayonnaise.

Now blend in the sour cream and then the half-and-half. Add the optional lemon juice for a more pronounced lemon flavor. If the dressing is a little too thick, add a little more half-and-half. Add a pinch of salt if needed. Keeps about 2 weeks in the fridge.

*Substitute pasteurized egg yolk if you wish.

Lemon Mayo Dressing

This delicious and zesty lemon dressing works wonders drizzled over a simple wedge of iceberg lettuce, sliced tomatoes, and sliced cucumbers. I also like to use it to bring zing to any kind of sandwich.

Makes 1¼ cup

1 cup mayonnaise
1 tablespoon sour cream
2 teaspoons finely grated lemon zest

1 tablespoon freshly squeezed lemon juice
1 tablespoon freshly squeezed orange juice
⅛ teaspoon freshly ground black pepper

To make the dressing

Put all of the ingredients into a small mixing bowl and whisk together until totally blended. Store in a covered container in the fridge for 2 weeks.

Creamy Mustard Dressing

This dressing is direct from The Copper Kettle, 1969, Aspen, Colorado. It's included here because I still love it and still make it at my restaurant. I also include it to remember Sarah Armstrong, mastermind of the Copper Kettle, in thanks for all she taught me.

Makes 1+ cups

2 hard-boiled eggs

1 teaspoon kosher salt

1¼ teaspoons sugar

1 teaspoon freshly ground black pepper

1 tablespoon chopped parsley

1 tablespoon Dijon mustard

1 large clove garlic, smashed and minced

¼ cup red wine vinegar

½ cup light olive oil

4 tablespoons whole milk

To make the dressing

Add the first 9 ingredients to a blender and, with the lid on, blend till smooth. Now while blending, add in the milk in a steady stream until fully incorporated. Taste for seasoning. Dressing will keep covered for 2 weeks in the fridge.

Honey-Mustard Mayo Dressing

This dressing comes from the spicy and exotic cooking of Cuba via Miami. It is called Nuevo Cubano and works great on Nuevo Cubano sandwiches— ham, roast pork, cheese, lettuce, and some of this dressing will transport you right to Miami Beach.

Makes about 1¼ cup

1 tablespoon orange juice
1 tablespoon honey
1 cup mayonnaise

2 tablespoons mustard
⅛ teaspoon freshly ground black pepper

To make the dressing

In a mixing bowl add the orange juice and the honey. Stir until the honey dissolves. Add the mayonnaise and mustard. My favorite mustards are deli, Dijon, or coarse country mustard. Whisk to blend evenly and then whisk in the black pepper. Store in a covered container in the fridge for 2 weeks.

Curried Honey-Orange Mayo

We get a little Middle Eastern essence with this dressing. It works great in apple chicken salad for a pita sandwich or tossed into a fruit salad. Or just dollop a spoonful over a piece of grilled salmon.

Makes about 1¼ cup

1 tablespoon freshly squeezed orange juice
½ teaspoon freshly squeezed lemon juice
2 teaspoons honey
1 cup mayonnaise

1 tablespoon sour cream
1¼ teaspoons curry powder
2 teaspoons finely grated orange zest
⅛ teaspoon freshly ground black pepper

To make the dressing

In a mixing bowl, add the orange juice, lemon juice, and honey, and stir until the honey dissolves. Now add the remaining ingredients and whisk until they are evenly blended. Stores in a covered container in the fridge for 2 weeks.

Variation: Curried Honey-Orange with Toasted-Almond Mayo Dressing

I love the toasty and nutty flavor the almonds add to this dressing. This is a simple case of taking something really good one step farther.

Make the Curried Honey-Orange Mayo, then stir in ¼ cup lightly toasted slivered almonds.

Avocado Mayo Dressing

One of my favorite taste combinations in the world is avocado, fresh lime juice, hot chili sauce, and a little salt and pepper. I love to eat avocados in just this simple way. This combo is my theme for the creation of this dressing. I use it to dollop on street tacos, as a dressing over a combination of Latino salads, or as a dollop on a grilled Gaucho steak or spicy grilled chicken sliced over greens. This is easy and fast to make, so give it a try.

Makes about 1 cup

1 ripe medium avocado, peeled and pitted
½ cup mayonnaise
1 tablespoon sour cream
1 tablespoon plus 1 teaspoon
    freshly squeezed lime juice
1 teaspoon Dijon mustard

1 tablespoon chopped cilantro leaves
1 teaspoon hot chili sauce (my favorites
    are Tabasco and Sriracha)
⅛ teaspoon freshly ground black pepper
⅛ teaspoon kosher salt

To make the dressing

In a mixing bowl, use a fork to mash the avocado. Add the remaining ingredients and mix until blended. I like the dressing to be a little coarse, not too smooth. This dressing is made to be used right away. Avocado is very perishable. If there is some left over, you can put it in a small bowl or cup and squeeze some lime juice over it, which will keep the avocado from discoloring. But it is best to use immediately.

Spicy New Orleans Mayo

This is one of my favorite concoctions. It's New Orleans because of the mixture of celery, onions, bell pepper, and my Vintage Spice Mix. It works great with shellfish so use it with a crab salad, or try it on a lobster roll or shrimp sandwich. It also works great to spice up a Shrimp Louis Salad.

Makes about 1¼ cups

1 cup mayonnaise
1 teaspoon Vintage Spice Mix (page 58)
2 tablespoons finely minced celery

2 tablespoons finely minced red bell pepper
2 tablespoons finely minced sweet onion

To make the dressing

In a mixing bowl, stir together all the ingredients until well blended. Best used within one week to keep vegetables crunchy.

Peppery Country-Mustard Mayo

I love this mayo for potato salad. Be sure to include chopped hard-boiled egg, diced celery, diced onion, and crispy bacon in the potato salad. This tangy mayo will bring out all the flavors. Another alternative is to add some chopped dill pickle to the dressing and then use it for tuna salad, chicken salad, or egg salad. A spoonful of this dressing over freshly grilled fish is wonderful.

Makes about 1½ cups

1 cup mayonnaise

2 tablespoons sour cream

1 tablespoon plus 1 teaspoon
    coarse country mustard

2 tablespoons finely diced shallots

1 teaspoon finely diced garlic

¼ teaspoon freshly ground black pepper

1 tablespoon white wine vinegar

1 tablespoon freshly snipped tarragon or dill

To make the dressing

Put all of the ingredients into a mixing bowl and blend with a whisk until evenly mixed. Best used within 1 week.

Honey-Orange Dressing for Fruit Salad

My mom made this dressing every holiday season for her amazing molded fruit-and-nut Jell-O salads. This is the essence of simplicity. So use it like my mom did or as a dressing for a mixed fruit salad.

Makes about 1¼ cups

1 tablespoon honey
1 tablespoon freshly squeezed orange juice

1 cup good-quality plain yogurt
1 teaspoon finely grated orange zest

To make the dressing

In a bowl, dissolve the honey in the orange juice. Now mix in the yogurt and orange zest until they are evenly blended. Best used within 3 days.

Spicy Cucumber, Dill, and Yogurt Dressing

For a most refreshing taste on a hot summer day, use a yogurt dressing on a salad. They are light vibrant dressings and quick and simple to put together. This one is especially good drizzled over a wedge of lettuce with your favorite veggie additions.

Makes about 2 cups

1 cup good-quality plain yogurt
3/4 cup peeled, seeded, and sliced cucumber
1 tablespoon freshly chopped dill
1 teaspoon minced jalapeno pepper
1/2 teaspoon minced garlic
1 tablespoon minced shallot or onion

1 tablespoon freshly squeezed orange juice
1 tablespoon extra virgin olive oil
1/8 teaspoon freshly ground black pepper
1 pinch cayenne
1 pinch kosher salt

To make the dressing

Put all of the ingredients into a food processor and pulse the mixture until it is ground evenly into a nice texture. Best used within 3 days.

Curried Orange-and-Mint Yogurt Dressing

This yogurt dressing has a Middle Eastern quality with the curry, orange, and mint combination. I make it with cucumber to give it a textural quality. I like this dressing drizzled over couscous salad with tomatoes, sliced onions, and roasted chicken. It is also wonderful tossed with watercress, fresh orange segments, and sweet onion slices for a salad that will stand alone. Or serve it over freshly grilled sea bass or other white-fleshed fish filets.

Makes about 1½ cups

1 tablespoon honey
1 tablespoon orange juice
1 cup good-quality plain yogurt
½ cup peeled, seeded, and
    chopped cucumber
1½ tablespoons thinly sliced fresh mint leaves

½ teaspoon smashed and diced garlic
1 teaspoon finely grated orange zest
⅛ teaspoon freshly ground black pepper
1 teaspoon curry powder
1 pinch kosher salt to taste

To make the dressing

First, dissolve the honey with the orange juice in a cup. Put this mixture into a food processor along with all the rest of the ingredients and pulse the mixture until it has a perfect dressing texture. Best used within 3 days.

Buttermilk Blue Cheese Dressing

Here is a tangy take on creamy blue cheese dressing. Use drizzled over wedges of lettuce, tossed with a favorite mixed salad blend, or drizzled over grilled summer shish kebabs for a real treat.

Makes about 1 cup

½ cup buttermilk

2 tablespoons sour cream

⅓ cup crumbled blue cheese

¼ teaspoon minced garlic

1 teaspoon finely minced shallot

1 teaspoon freshly squeezed lemon juice

1 tablespoon extra virgin olive oil

Freshly ground black pepper to taste

Kosher salt to taste

To make the dressing

Put the first 7 ingredients into a mixing bowl and whisk until evenly blended. Add a pinch of pepper and a pinch of salt and taste. Add more if needed or desired. Store in the fridge and use within 1 week.

Spicy Buttermilk Fresh Herb Dressing

A light, cool, and refreshing dressing for a summer-day salad.

Makes about 1 cup

½ cup buttermilk

4 tablespoons sour cream

¼ teaspoon smashed and minced garlic

1 teaspoon finely minced red onion

1 tablespoon freshly squeezed orange juice

1 teaspoon freshly squeezed lemon juice

1 tablespoon extra virgin olive oil

⅛ teaspoon cayenne

1 tablespoon chopped fresh herb of your
   choice, such as dill, parsley, or chervil

Kosher salt and freshly ground
   black pepper to taste

To make the dressing

Put all of the ingredients into a mixing
bowl and whisk until evenly blended. Use
within 1 week. Store in fridge.

Cowboy Buttermilk Ranch Dressing

Here's one to use when you are having a real ranch BBQ. Just make a big bowl of mixed greens and toss with this dressing. Or slather it on steaming corn on the cob. Better yet, add some crumbled blue cheese to the dressing and drizzle it over the BBQ meats and grilled veggies you are cooking. Yum, yum, yum!

Makes about 1 cup

½ cup ranch dressing
1 tablespoon sour cream
½ teaspoon minced garlic
⅓ cup buttermilk

1 tablespoon extra virgin olive oil
1 teaspoon freshly squeezed lime juice
½ to 1 teaspoon Vintage Spice Mix (page 58)
⅓ cup crumbled blue cheese (optional)

To make the dressing

Put all of the ingredients into a mixing bowl and whisk till evenly blended. Store covered in the fridge; use within 1 week.

French Dijon Mustard Dressing

This little dressing is simple and fast. It's one of the flavors that we like to call the taste of France.

Makes about ¾ cup

1 tablespoon Dijon mustard
2 tablespoons red wine vinegar
1 tablespoon freshly squeezed lemon juice
1 small clove garlic, smashed and minced

⅓ cup extra virgin olive oil
Small pinch kosher salt, or to taste
Pinch freshly ground black pepper

To make the dressing

In a small mixing bowl, add the mustard, vinegar, lemon juice and garlic. Swirl with a whisk to combine well. Add the oil in a light, steady stream, whisking. The dressing will blend nicely. Taste for salt and pepper.

If it is your pleasure, throw in a tablespoon of one of your favorite chopped fresh herbs. This dressing is perfect for mixed green salads, drizzled on sandwiches or drizzled over a plate of sliced tomatoes, sliced sweet onions, sliced mozzarella and freshly snipped basil. Enjoy!

MIX-IN DRESSINGS

MIX-IN SALAD DRESSINGS are custom-made dressings that are quick and easy to put together because you buy a bottled dressing at the market and then customize it with added ingredients that you mix in to enhance the flavor, creating a simple and unique dressing of your own.

I got this idea from my mom one night while having dinner at her house years ago. She served a mixed green salad with a delicious creamy Asian dressing. I gave her a huge compliment on the salad, and she asked if I wanted to know her secret. "Of course," was my quick response. "Well, Jeff," she said, "It's so easy!" She went on to explain that she had bought a commercial bottled salad dressing, mixed in some other ingredients, and came up with the creamy Asian dressing that she had just served. It is a great idea, and her dressing was delicious and very unique. So let's get started with none other than my mother's Creamy Asian Salad Dressing.

Creamy Asian Salad Dressing

This is my mom's original mix-in dressing. She was great at thinking up new taste treats.

I'll never forget her delight when we liked what she made.

Makes about 2 cups

1 (13-ounce) bottle Soy Vay Cha-Cha Chinese Chicken Salad Dressing
¾ cup Nasoya Nayonnaise

1 teaspoon lightly toasted sesame seeds
2 tablespoons Asian-style, diagonally thin-sliced green onions

To make the dressing

Put all of the ingredients into a mixing bowl and whisk together until thoroughly blended. Stores in a covered container for 2 weeks in the fridge. This dressing works great with green salad blends or with Asian noodle salads.

Chipotle-Lime Ranch Dressing

This one is warm (bordering on hot), smokey with a light tang, and creamy. It's a nice combo for south-of-the-border combos of mixed greens with lots of tomatoes. It's also great drizzled on grilled veggies or corn on the cob, or as a dip for veggie sticks or grilled bread. It's a good sauce for steak and chicken too.

Makes 1 cup

1½ teaspoons Embasa brand chipotle chili with adobo sauce

1 cup bottled Hidden Valley Ranch Dressing
3 teaspoons freshly squeezed lime juice

To make the dressing

Take one chipotle pepper, cut it in half, and scrape out the seeds. Discard the seeds and chop up the pepper. Then, in a mixing bowl, add the ranch dressing, the chipotle pepper with some of the adobo sauce, and the lime juice; whisk together until blended evenly. Use more or less chipotle and adobo depending on how strong and hot you want the dressing. Keeps in the fridge in a covered container for 10 days.

Creamy Wasabi Salad Dressing

This is a nice variation on Mom's original mix-in dressing. It packs a lot of heat, so get ready for an endorphin rush.

Makes about 2 ¼ cups

1 (13-ounce) bottle Soy Vay Cha-Cha Chinese Chicken Salad Dressing
¾ cup Dynasty Wasabi Mayonnaise

2 tablespoons Asian-style, diagonally thin-sliced green onions

To make the dressing

Put all of the ingredients into a mixing bowl and whisk together until blended evenly. Stores in a covered container for 2 weeks in the fridge. This dressing works great with green salad blends or with Asian noodle salads.

Creamy Sesame Ginger Salad Dressing

I'm glad that I discovered Bragg's Apple Cider Vinegar and salad dressing products. They are all about healthy and vital living. This dressing is a total energy booster.

Makes about 1¼ cups

1 (12-ounce) bottle Bragg Ginger
    & Sesame Salad Dressing
¾ cup Nasoya Nayonnaise
1 tablespoon chopped green onion

1 tablespoon lightly toasted sesame seeds
1 teaspoon finely minced garlic
1 tablespoon finely grated fresh ginger

To make the dressing

Put all of the ingredients into a mixing bowl and whisk until evenly blended. Stores for 2 weeks in the fridge in a covered container. This dressing is great with Asian salad green blends or with cold Asian noodle salads.

Tomato Ranch Dressing

This recipe idea comes from my great friend and food co-conspirator Candy Durham. Candy has a wonderful feel for food and never fails to come up with great ideas. This is one of her best ever, and it has stayed in my restaurant repertoire. It is not only a great salad dressing but also a fabulous dip for veggies and a spread for sandwiches.

Makes about 3 cups

1 (24-ounce) bottle Hidden Valley Ranch Dressing

²/₃ cup good-quality prepared chili sauce

³/₄ cup crumbled blue cheese

To make the dressing

Put all of the ingredients into a food processor and pulse until thoroughly blended. Store in a covered container in the fridge for up to 10 days. Cut the recipe in half if this is too much dressing for what you need.

Cowboy Thousand Island Ranch Dressing

If you have a little cowboy spirit buried somewhere inside, this dressing will appeal to you.

Makes 4 cups

1 (24-ounce) bottle Hidden
  Valley Ranch Dressing
1/3 cup smokey barbeque sauce
3/4 cup crumbled blue cheese
2 teaspoons Embasa brand chipotle
  chili with adobo sauce

1 teaspoon freshly squeezed lime juice
3 hard-boiled eggs, chopped medium
1/3 cup drained and chopped dill pickle

To make the dressing

Put the first 5 ingredients into a food processor and pulse until everything is evenly blended. Then pour the dressing into a bowl and stir in the chopped egg and pickles. Keeps in a covered container in the fridge for 10 days.

Texan Barbeque Ranch Dressing

Here is a smokey Texas twist to Tomato Ranch Dressing. It's great whenever you cook outdoors. Try slathering it on corn on the cob.

Makes about 3½ cups

1 (24-ounce) bottle Hidden
   Valley Ranch Dressing
⅓ cup smokey barbeque sauce
¾ cup crumbled blue cheese

2 teaspoons Embasa brand canned
   chipotle chili with adobo sauce
2 teaspoons freshly squeezed lime juice

To make the dressing

Put all of the ingredients into a food processor and pulse until evenly blended. Keep in a covered container in the fridge for 10 days. Cut the recipe in half if this is too much for what you need.

INDEX

Acknowledgments

A hearty thank-you goes to Gibbs Smith for giving me the opportunity to create this book. Gibbs is an explorer of ideas to help create a better world and for that alone it is a privilege to know him. To Jennifer Adams, my editor, walking down the path to create a new book with you is always a pleasure. And to my family and crew at Vintage Restaurant, my deepest thanks for your unconditional support and for your tolerance of my long silences while working on the book.

Metric Conversion Chart

Volume Measurements		Weight Measurements		Temperature Conversion	
U.S.	Metric	U.S.	Metric	Fahrenheit	Celsius
1 teaspoon	5 ml	½ ounce	15 g	250	120
1 tablespoon	15 ml	1 ounce	30 g	300	150
¼ cup	60 ml	3 ounces	90 g	325	160
⅓ cup	75 ml	4 ounces	115 g	350	180
½ cup	125 ml	8 ounces	225 g	375	190
⅔ cup	150 ml	12 ounces	350 g	400	200
¾ cup	175 ml	1 pound	450 g	425	220
1 cup	250 ml	2¼ pounds	1 kg	450	230